HISTORIC PHOTOS OF
OKLAHOMA LAWMEN

TEXT AND CAPTIONS BY LARRY JOHNSON

TURNER
PUBLISHING COMPANY

Deputy U.S. Marshal Robert Galbreath (1863–1953) stands near his headquarters in Edmond in 1890. A former associate of Boomers, Galbreath was the embodiment of Oklahoma's early development, having been an 1889er, a marshal, a postmaster, a judge, and finally co-discoverer of the Glenn Pool as an oilman.

ACKNOWLEDGMENTS

This volume, *Historic Photos of Oklahoma Lawmen,* is the result of the cooperation and efforts of many individuals, organizations, and corporations. It is with great thanks that we acknowledge the valuable contribution of the following for their generous support:

Fort Smith National Historic Site

Museum of the Great Plains

Oklahoma Historical Society

Plains Indians & Pioneers Museum

Terry Lamar Collection

Waynoka Historical Society

Western History Collection, University of Oklahoma

The author would like to thank Debra Spindle and Beverly Mosman at the Oklahoma Historical Society, Alexandra Shadid at the University of Oklahoma's Western History Collection, Deborah Anna Baroff at the Museum of the Great Plains, Sandra Olson at the Waynoka Historical Society, and Terry Lamar for their wonderful assistance in researching photographs for this book.

Thanks to Doug Bentin for moral support and reality checking.

With the exception of touching up imperfections that have accrued with the passage of time and cropping where necessary, no changes have been made. The focus and clarity of many images is limited by the technology and the ability of the photographer at the time they were taken.

PREFACE

During a recent discussion of the state of publishing in Oklahoma, a historian at the state's largest university proclaimed, "The last thing we need is another book on outlaws and lawmen." He makes a valid point; the topic has been well covered in hundreds of books by everyone from the scholarly historian to the bolo-wearing amateur.

So here's one more book. But this book tells the story of Oklahoma's lawmen in the lines of their faces and the cut of their coat. Here are the baby-faced and the grizzled; eyes who've seen too much of this world and the look of false bravado; some in their native costume and others in their dress blues.

Depicted here is a fascinating visual representation of the early history of Oklahoma lawmen, and the selection of photographs here tells the story of a diverse group of people who shared the same profession. It begins with the ranging mounted cavalry brought to the eastern part of the state by the Five Civilized Tribes and the scouts and Dog Soldiers in the west. Federal marshals gradually appear as the presence of white intruders grows in the Indian nations, to be followed by the county sheriff, the policeman, and the prohibition agent. Readers will also see that the lawmen bringing justice to Oklahoma had to navigate a dizzying array of jurisdictions and often moved back and forth between them; at times some even held simultaneous positions like Indian Policeman and Deputy U.S. Marshal.

Equally diverse are the uniforms and tools of the lawmen. Some of the tribal lawmen, especially the United States Indian Police, wore cavalry-style uniforms, whole others wore more traditional clothing, and some are seen here with traditional weapons in addition to the carbine and pistol. Federal marshals and most county sheriffs are likewise seen in contemporary clothing with pistols slung at the hip, while the policemen are always uniformed. The symbol that unifies them all, however, is the badge, and the reader will see a wide array of badges ranging from star to shield.

There are plenty of photographs of lawmen executing their duties as well. The reader will see illegal white settlers ejected by Indian police; prisoners escorted by marshals; patrolmen on horseback, astride motorcycles, and behind the wheel of a car; and the confiscation and destruction of moonshine stills and their products.

—Larry Johnson

Marshal Bat Masterson hired Bill Tilghman as his deputy in Dodge City, Kansas, where the two went about bringing law and order to the ferocious cowtown. Here, Tilghman appears during his own stint as city marshal in the mid-1880s.

LET NO GUILTY MAN ESCAPE

(1870s–1889)

When the Five Civilized Tribes were forcibly removed from their homes and resettled in the Indian Territory in the 1830s, they brought with them an intact justice system and definite ideas of law enforcement and punishment. To enforce the laws, each tribe had a mounted force called Light Horse, named for Revolutionary War hero General Henry "Lighthorse Harry" Lee, which drew men from each district led by a captain. The main force normally only comprised between 10 and 20 men, but could swell in times of emergency. Later, district sheriffs were added in the most populous areas.

Duties of the Light Horse included the usual peace keeping common to all police forces, but they were also responsible for the administration of justice. The tribes held that imprisonment was too great a punishment for anyone, so minor offenses were punished with up to 100 lashes and major offenses met death by rifle shot. Both of these were duties executed by the Light Horse.

As the population grew in the nations and the railroads entered the territory, more whites began to enter the country legally and illegally. They were not bound by tribal law however, so in 1851 the federal court in Fort Smith, Arkansas, was given jurisdiction over whites in the Indian Territory. In 1875, the "hangin' judge" Isaac C. Parker famously took the bench and meted out swift, harsh justice, ultimately executing 79 people. Though few in number during this period, United States marshals did have authority in the nations in regard to the affairs of whites and had free range over the territory to execute their duties.

In the west, several nomadic tribes were relocated to the territory during the Indian Wars of the 1870s. These tribes also had mounted police forces, though they tended to appear more military in structure. Some tribes, like the Kiowa, called them scouts, but the Cheyenne were called Dog Soldiers (this was a generic name applied by outsiders—the Cheyenne had six military societies in their tribe, only one of which went by the name Dog).

Finally, in 1880, the United States Indian Police service was formed to assist Indian Agents in executing their duties. These were also a mounted force attached to each agency and generally made up of members of the tribe. Theirs was a precarious position as they were often shunned by their own people for executing the laws of an occupying force and an alien culture.

Jim Elder (at left) and future law enforcement legend Bill Tilghman as teenaged buffalo hunters pose for a photograph around the 1870s. The pair claimed to have killed thousands of bison in the West over a three-year period.

Seen here as a young Indian Policeman, Black Coyote or Wa-tan-gaa was a remarkable example of the dual lives many Indians lived in Oklahoma. Not only was Black Coyote a captain of the police, a delegate to Washington, and a wealthy farmer, he also aspired to be a great priest and medicine man.

After the majority of the Seminole tribe sided with the Confederacy in 1861, John Chupco (seated, center) led his people to Kansas to join loyalist Creeks in the Indian Home Guard Brigade. After the Civil War he was recognized as chief of the reunited tribe and as such led the Seminole Light Horse seen here. The Light Horse themselves were not exclusively Indian. The forces included some blacks—freed slaves owned by Indians before the Civil War—and some whites through marriage to Indian women.

Undoubtedly one of the most colorful figures in Oklahoma history was Zeke Proctor, around whom the Going Snake Massacre of 1872—actually an epic gun battle in which eight deputy U.S. marshals were killed—was centered. For most of his life he was called an outlaw, but after receiving a pardon from President Grant, he became a Cherokee sheriff and a two-term deputy U.S. marshal.

Appointed in 1873, Deputy U.S. Marshal Ben Williams maintained order in the Cheyenne and Arapaho country, driving out such white intruders as horse thieves and whiskey peddlers. The son of Quakers, Williams reportedly "revolted at killing a fellow man but it was woe betide the man who made the killing obligatory."

Ohioan Isaac C. Parker was named to the bench of the Western District of Arkansas and Indian Territory in 1875 by fellow Buckeye Ulysses S. Grant. To tame the wild country, Parker struck quickly and hard by holding mass hangings early on, earning him the sobriquet "Hangin' Judge."

Ex-slave Bass Reeves was one of the first deputy marshals hired by Judge Isaac Parker's court—and he was one of the judge's favorites. Over a 30-year career, he nabbed 3,000 badmen. In 1902, he even had to bring in his own son, who was tried and convicted of murder and sent to a federal prison.

Already a veteran of wars in Denmark, Algeria, and France when he arrived in America in 1876, future Oklahoma law enforcement legend Chris Madsen joined the U.S. Army to fight Indians in the West. Here he is seen in his late 20s as an Indian Scout in the Cavalry where he served alongside Buffalo Bill. In 1898, Madsen joined up with Teddy Roosevelt's Rough Riders, and would attempt to enlist in the army at the outset of World War I, but he was rejected because of his age.

Just before Christmas in 1886, Cherokee Sam Sixkiller, captain of the U.S. Indian Police and a deputy marshal, was gunned down by outlaw Dick Vann. Sixkiller was much beloved by those "down in the Nation" and was perhaps the best-known Cherokee in the United States.

Sankadota was a member of the elite Qoichegau military society among the Kiowa, and the Indian agent in Anadarko turned to him to be captain of his tribe's contingent of the U.S. Indian Police when it was formed in 1880.

Pleasant Luther "Duke" Berryhill came from a prominent Creek family in the Okmulgee area and served in the Creek Light Horse for many years, 16 of them as captain of the Light Horse. As the ranking law enforcement official in the Creek Nation, he meted out punishments sent down by the tribal court in Okmulgee.

Timmie Jack (at left) and James Brown (right) pose with their wives (and an unidentified woman, at center). On New Year's Eve 1886, a drunken Timmie killed his friend James with a knife for which the tribal council sentenced him to death by rifle shot. As was custom, he selected his own executioner—Light Horse captain Duke Berryhill, his best friend.

The court of Indian offenses in the Ponca Nation, around the 1880s. The agent assigned to the tribe reported that the three Ponca judges "feel the dignity of their position and display much judgment and seem willing and anxious to conform to the law."

A member of the Indian Police near the tribal court at the Ponca Agency, around the 1880s. An eastern observer reported that the Ponca police force "has not only been most efficacious in the maintenance of law and order, but also in producing a moral discipline formerly unknown to them."

Belle Starr in Fort Smith not long after she was brought into court by Deputy Marshal Tyner Hughes (at right) on a robbery charge in 1886. Belle was caught off guard by Hughes and was quoted (perhaps apocryphally) as saying, "Hughes is a brave man and acted the gentleman in every particular, but I hardly believed he realized his danger."

During his 20-year career as a deputy U.S. marshal, which began in the 1880s, Joe Payne "knew the Cherokee country better than a full-blood Indian" and was known for often working alone. Perhaps those two factors are what makes the legend of his lost silver strike in the Oklahoma Ozarks so intriguing to treasure hunters today.

Anadarko's sheriff and his deputies prepare to ride, around the 1880s. Anadarko was quite busy as the key settlement in southwestern Oklahoma, and regular traffic by soldiers from Fort Sill and Indian encampments nearby ensured that these officers rarely had a quiet day.

An Indian Police encampment near Anadarko, around the 1880s. The United States Indian Police wore the badge for the Cherokee, Choctaw, Chickasaw, Creek, and Seminole in pursuit of Indian bad guys and others.

A one-time member of a Boomer colony, sturdily built Harry L. Strough found employment as a deputy U.S. marshal two months before the land run of 1889. He spent the remainder of his service evicting Sooners and settling claims disputes.

Jailers and guards, with hangman George Maledon likely the man in the center, stand on the steps of the Federal Courthouse in Fort Smith, around 1889.

After years of intensive lobbying by Cherokee Elias Boudinot and others, a federal court was finally established in Indian Territory in March 1889—just a month before the first of the great land runs. Though it acknowledged the growing importance of Muskogee, the facilities were nonetheless inauspicious.

Unlike their U.S. Indian Police counterparts, these Cheyenne-Arapaho Scouts attached to Fort Reno were not officially called police, but they performed many policing duties, including arresting and detaining intruders. These Scouts are posing for a photograph in 1889.

Illinois banker Thomas B. Needles was appointed the first U.S. marshal of Indian Territory in 1889 and worked out of the new federal court in Muskogee. Among his many memorable actions in Oklahoma was his decision to end self-rule in unorganized Oklahoma City in December 1889.

The Stern Hand of Civilization Will Crush the Wilderness Out

(1889–1899)

As the states surrounding Indian Territory began to fill with settlers, pressure increased on the established nations in the territory. White boomers began to pressure the federal government to open land up to settlement, and many began making illegal attempts to settle. Incursions by ranchers and their cattle, whiskey peddlers, and black marketers also increased. The most troubling development was the arrival of the criminal element as a great many fugitives from the United States headed for the Indian Territory to hide or to execute their nefarious activities unhindered by tribal justice systems, which could do nothing legally to stop them.

Previously, the courts at Fort Smith, Arkansas; Wichita, Kansas; and Paris, Texas, dispatched deputy marshals into the nations to apprehend fugitives, but when it was decided to allow white settlement and later to dismantle tribal governments under the Dawes (1893) and Curtis (1898) acts, more federal courts were established with the first at Muskogee in 1889.

This period was the golden age of law enforcement in Oklahoma, when United States marshals and their deputies aggressively pursued their quarry in the face of hardship and danger all the while riding into the history books to be romanticized and adored for generations. The most famous men of this period included Marshal Evett Nix' Three Guardsmen: Bill Tilghman, Heck Thomas, and Chris Madsen. And while these men were impeccably forthright, many in their number walked both sides of the line, finding they could make more money on the other side of the law.

If the marshals represent the romanticized notion of the West, in Oklahoma the Wild West often clashed with civilization on city streets. While most of its neighbors took decades to develop urban concentrations, Oklahoma could number many sizable cities in its territory overnight. Oklahoma City, for example, was born in 1889 with 10,000 residents, and quickly established a police force.

Also entering the law enforcement community during this period are the county sheriffs, who executed a variety of duties including serving court papers, selling seized property, and patrolling outlying areas of their jurisdictions.

As tribal governments declined in this period, the Light Horse also diminished. Most tribes, however, now have tribal police forces that grew out of these pioneer police forces.

Political appointee Warren Lurty of Virginia quickly ran afoul of thousands of ex-Kansans after his appointment as first U.S. marshal of Oklahoma Territory in May of 1890. Though the public squabble was over his former status as a Confederate, it was his political patronage that forced him to retire in July of that year.

This scene in Guthrie just after the destruction of a supply of liquor by U.S. marshals was photographed in May 1889. Contrary to public opinion, the government considered the newly opened land in Oklahoma still a part of Indian Territory, where liquor was forbidden. When Oklahoma Territory was formed in 1890, prohibition was removed.

Defenders of civilized society stand in front of the City Marshal's office in Guthrie in 1889, where lawmen Ed P. Kelly and J. V. Leis maintained law and order. Though the quality of their work seems impeccable, Walker & McCoy had room for improvement as spellers as evidenced by the extra "L" on the sign of their neighbor.

Ed P. Kelly made a career of being trustworthy to powerful people. In 1889, he was the first city marshal of Guthrie and soon after one of the first deputy U.S. marshals of the new Oklahoma Territory, then clerk of the federal court, and finally the number-two man for the Rock Island Railroad.

The inaugural Oklahoma City Police Department, formed in August 1890 with the ubiquitous Charles Colcord (seated) as chief of police and mammoth John Hubatka behind him. At its official formation weeks earlier, Oklahoma City was divided into four wards with one policeman assigned to each ward.

Chief of Osage Police Morris Robacker (standing, at right) appears with his officers around 1890 not long after the post was relinquished by the soon-to-be notorious outlaw Bob Dalton, who was fired for importing whiskey into the Osage Nation.

An unidentified deputy U.S. marshal sits for a
photograph around the 1890s.

Peyote fan in hand, a Comanche
Indian Policeman takes time for a
photograph in 1890. Comanche
policemen were active in border patrol
along the Red River and evicted
prospectors bent on extracting gold
from the Wichita Mountains.

Pawnee Indian Police at the Pawnee Agency, 1891. The Pawnee were noted in the era for their acceptance of law and order. The police spent most of their efforts vigilantly patrolling their borders and chasing out white hunters and other intruders.

Deputy U.S. Marshal George Thornton, around 1890. A year later he was ambushed by outlaws near the Sac and Fox Agency. He and a posseman were attacked while trying to serve papers on Creek outlaw Captain Willie. Thornton suffered a fatal wound during the hail of bullets from unseen assailants.

Around 1890, Comanche Ar-ko sat for photographers in Purcell during his stint as a United States Indian Policeman (including service as captain) operating from the Kiowa Agency in Anadarko.

Kope-ta, an associate of Ar-ko on the Indian Police, sat for this photograph in 1890.

The assembled force of the Otoe Indian Police, around 1892. Although they were charged with carrying out the orders of both the Agency and the tribal court, Agent D. J. M. Wood complained, "I find it hard work to retain them in the service . . . they do not like to enforce an order when it conflicts with tribal customs."

The Guthrie office of the Western District, around 1891. Some of Oklahoma's most famous and admired lawmen worked from this office. Notable in this image are Marshal William Grimes (seated, third from left), and deputies Chris Madsen (seated, at left) and Heck Thomas (standing, at left).

Deputy U.S. Marshals John Swain (at left) and Matt Cook, 1892. Swain operated primarily in the Chickasaw Nation in the 1890s, but lost his commission after fellow deputy E. H. Scrivener testified that Swain doubled as ringleader of a band of cattle thieves. Soon after, Swain was gunned down by men he had been feuding with.

U.S. Marshal William Grimes presides over admission to the Kingfisher land office during the opening of the Cheyenne-Arapaho lands in 1892. Grimes was there to keep the peace, but created unrest when he began assigning places at the front of the line for speculators.

The assembled deputies of the court at Paris, Texas, in 1892, most notably Heck Thomas (seated, second from right) and Chris Madsen (directly behind Thomas). The men of this jurisdiction had to root their quarry from the thickly wooded mountains of the Choctaw Nation.

One of the more enduring controversies in Oklahoma history is the case of Cherokee outlaw Ned Christie, framed for the murder of Deputy U.S. Marshal Daniel Maples in 1887. Christie went on the lam, evading authorities for five years before his death in a shoot-out in 1892. He was exonerated 30 years later.

Deputy Marshal Paden Tolbert (front, center) led this posse, which made the final assault on fugitive Ned Christie's hilltop fortress in the Cookson Hills. The lawmen used a cannon and dynamite during the two-day siege to blast Christie out of his refuge. The outlaw was finally gunned down as he fled the burning cabin.

The wild ride of two of the Dalton boys, Bob (left) and Grat (right), ended in a bloody shoot-out with townsfolk in Coffeyville, Kansas, in 1892. Long the foil of some of the best U.S. marshals, the Daltons had an edge in evading their hunters. In the late 1880s, they had been marshals themselves.

Prisoners kneel before their Choctaw Light Horse captors in March 1893, during the infamous Locke-Jones War. After a disputed election for chief, rival factions fought open battles and though the Light Horse were somewhat involved in the events, they eventually brought order to the troubled nation.

Choctaw Light Horsemen prepare for a skirmish at Antlers in 1893. These men were likely involved in the Locke-Jones War.

A change in the administration of Indian affairs in 1894 saw the replacement of non-military Indian agents by Army officers. Here new agent Lieutenant Maury Nichols is seen leading the detachment of Indian Police from the agency in Anadarko. Nichols was no match for the powerful Comanche Quanah Parker and lasted only a year.

In March 1893, Congress authorized the purchase of roughly 8 million acres of land known as the Cherokee Outlet from the Cherokee tribe for the sum of $8,595,736.12. The down payment of $293,876 was received in cash, with the balance to be paid annually over five years. Here the Cherokee Light Horse guards a cash payment at Fort Gibson.

At 32, Guthrie businessman Evett Dumas Nix became the youngest U.S. marshal to hold the office in 1893. He assembled a formidable force of deputies to aggressively attack the criminal element rampaging Oklahoma Territory, most notably the Doolin-Dalton Gang.

Embodying one-third of Marshal E. D. Nix's Three Guardsmen, Heck Thomas was no stranger to danger. He had served as a 12-year-old Confederate soldier and an 18-year-old Atlanta policeman. As a deputy marshal in Oklahoma, first for Judge Parker, then for Nix, he was known as one of the most aggressive (and effective) manhunters on the force.

Deputy Marshal Heck Bruner worked for a time out of the Northern District in Vinita, where he seemed to have a nose for danger, having been involved in the capture of nearly every notorious outlaw gang nabbed in the 1890s. This patch of ground north of town is known as "Heck Bruner's Graveyard" and is filled with many of his quarry.

After chaos in 1889 and charges of fraud in 1892, Marshal E. D. Nix sent deputies Tilghman, Thomas, and Colcord (third from right) to the land office in Perry to police the line of homestead seekers during the Cherokee Outlet opening in September 1893.

Rising to a city of 25,000 people overnight after the Cherokee Outlet opening, Perry soon had 110 saloons and was frequented by outlaws like the Doolins and Daltons based in nearby Ingalls. Marshal Nix made the town a priority and assigned Guardsmen Thomas (at front, second from left) and Tilghman (seated, second from right) to tame it. Colcord was sent to Pawnee.

Two legendary Oklahoma figures, Deputy U.S. Marshal Bill Tilghman (left) and Deputy Charles Colcord, meet in 1893. Tilghman was in the midst of his assignment to clean up Perry while Colcord had been placed in charge of the Pawnee District by Marshal Nix.

Bill Painter served as Logan County Sheriff from 1892 to 1896 before setting out for the Yukon gold rush with Frank Canton. After his return, he was appointed the first sheriff of Comanche County. Unscrupulous, he tried to fix elections and it was said of him, "He was after all the money he could get out of the office."

Elected in 1894, Milton Jones would serve mere months of his term as Oklahoma City's chief of police. On June 30, 1895, three prisoners burst from the city jail and in the ensuing struggle over the getaway carriage, Jones was murdered in the street. He thus became the first Oklahoma City policeman to die in the line of duty.

"Old Reliable" John Vardeman was a deputy U.S. marshal for a time and later served as constable of Cleveland County. This image was recorded at the Maramec depot around 1894.

The last Choctaw execution took place at Wilburton on November 5, 1894. The victim was Silan Lewis, who was convicted of murder by the tribal court. After turning himself in (as was custom), he was shot through the chest at close range and then smothered as the mournful cry of a female relative arose from a nearby creek bank. Judge Holson of the Choctaw Criminal Court dissolved the Choctaw Light Horsemen in 1895, a decision that stemmed from the incident.

The scene at the Anadarko Indian Agency in 1894 features a smattering of Indian Police and their leader, Hummingbird (standing at center, with badge). Hummingbird was described by a newspaper reporter as "a fine, big fellow with all the dash of the savage in spite of the 'In God We Trust' buttons on the uniform."

Kiowa Indian Policeman Haumpy sits for a photograph in the 1890s. There is evidence to suggest that he may have been one of the last practitioners of buffalo medicine among the Kiowa people.

A U.S. Indian Policeman from the Darlington Agency (Cheyenne and Arapaho tribes) poses in El Reno around the 1890s. Liquor peddlers were the scourge of this agency and Indian Police routinely arrested them, but the courts assessed fines as small as one dollar, which hardly served to diminish sales.

"Fatty" Hopkins walked both sides of the line throughout his colorful career. Seen here in 1895 as an Oklahoma City cop, he later became quite wealthy bootlegging liquor to Indians while serving as a Lawton policeman. His head was split open with an ax in 1915 when his son sought to get a jump on his inheritance.

In 1894, Cherokee Bill (also known as Crawford Goldsby) joined with the Cook Gang on a crime spree in Indian Territory, murdering, robbing, and killing all in their path. Soon captured, after a year in prison he was executed by hanging. As the noose was put around his neck, Cherokee Bill told the crowd, "Today is as good a day to die as any."

During his imprisonment pending trial in 1895, Cherokee Bill surprised his jailers in an attempted escape. He shot jailer Lawrence Keating (seen here shortly before the events of July 10) in the stomach, and while Keating stumbled downstairs, Bill fatally shot him in the back. After an exchange of gunfire with other guards, Bill's ambitions to add "escaped prisoner" to his resume were foiled.

Austrian Gus Hadwiger was a deputy for both Woods County and Marshal Evett Nix in 1895. Operating out of Alva, he ranged in a large, sparsely populated area which included the Gloss Mountains, a haven for outlaws. Hadwiger later served in the Army in the Philippines Insurrection and finally became Woods County Judge in 1914.

Bill Fossett began his career in the notorious frontier town of Caldwell, Kansas, and later became a special agent for the Rock Island Railroad before signing on as a deputy U.S. marshal in 1895. After catching the eye of President Roosevelt, he was made U.S. marshal in 1902, a post he held for four years.

Two U.S. Indian Policemen from the Choctaw Nation stand for a photograph in the 1890s, with hands on their holstered guns.

Indian policemen Watchynunsukawa, Ah-ko (Comanches), and Charlie Buffalo (Kiowa) pose for a group shot at the Indian Agency in Anadarko. Watchynunsukawa, also known as Comanche Jack, may be the same man who later became a deputy U.S. marshal.

The Rufus Buck Gang embarked on a short-lived reign of terror in 1895 after the young group of mixed-blood Creeks and blacks joined forces to exact revenge on white intruders in the Creek Nation by way of murders and robberies. After killing an Okmulgee sheriff, they were apprehended by lawmen and the Creek Light Horse, tried, and hanged at the court in Fort Smith.

Deputy Marshal Bill Tilghman called gang leader Bill Doolin the "king" of Oklahoma's outlaws. He was captured by Tilghman in 1896, but made a break from the Guthrie jail before he could be brought to trial. Soon after, Heck Thomas tracked him down in Pawnee County, where Bill met the business end of a 10-gauge shotgun.

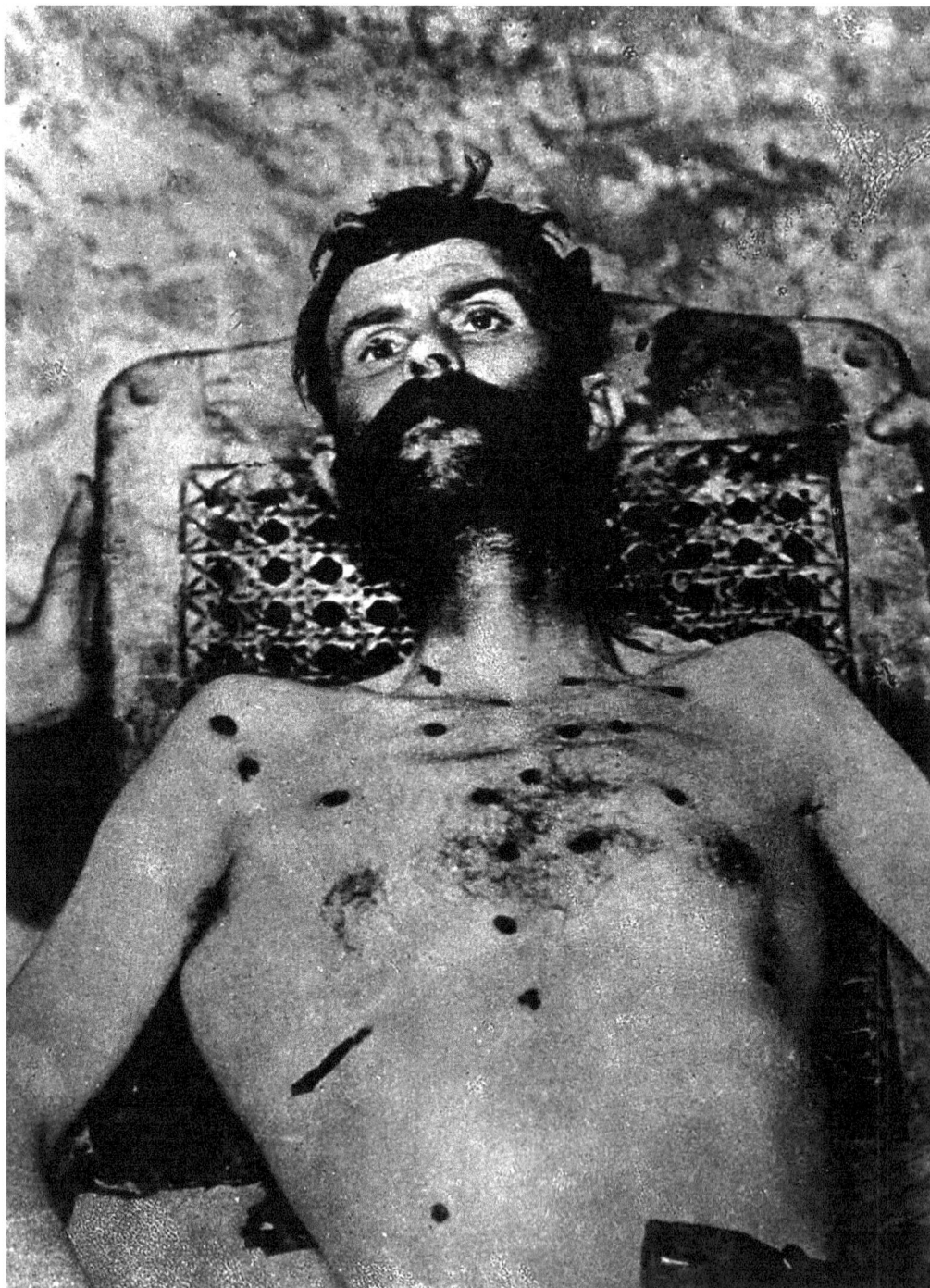

This image of a Dewey County sheriff's posse features "Uncle Joe" Ventioner on the right. Ventioner was once a tough deputy U.S. marshal who helped track down the Doolin Gang. He suffered and recovered from a serious abdomen wound during a shoot-out in 1896 in which he killed Red Buck, the man considered too wild for the Wild Bunch.

Sheriff of the Saline District, Cherokee Nation, Jess Sunday appears with his wife, Alice, shortly before passing the reins of the sheriff's office to his half brother Dave Ridge in 1897. In what became known as the "Saline Courthouse Massacre," a grocer named Baggett was murdered and Ridge and Sunday were killed during the investigation.

Pawnee County sheriff Frank Lake (seated at left) gave Frank Canton (seated with dog) an opportunity to salvage his life from its checkered past by making him a deputy. Seen here in 1897 with other deputies, the two tackled crime in this lawless area and made it "the most moral nook of the territory."

These men represented law and order in the Osage country as the twentieth century neared. Deputy U.S. Marshal Heck Thomas sits next to chief of Osage Indian Police Morris Robacker. Two Osage policemen are behind them, and clerk J. H. Havighorst and U.S. Attorney Roy Hoffman are in the back. This image was recorded around 1897.

Despite the best efforts of civilizing town officers like these men (the marshal stands at back, on the left), the little rail town of Caddo could be a dangerous place in 1896. As one of the few rail towns in the Indian Territory, it saw the comings and goings of many outlaws and marshals alike.

Deputy Marshals A. J. Trail (left) and Paden Tolbert (right) at the federal court in Muskogee. Both were well known in northeastern Oklahoma, where Tolbert led the efforts to capture outlaws Ned Christie, Texas Jack, and Al Jennings. Tolbert died young of kidney failure.

City Marshal James F. "Bud" Ledbetter on the beat in railroad town Vinita, 1899. Sometimes referred to as the Fourth Guardsman because of his close association with Marshal E. D. Nix's three more famous deputy U.S. marshals, Ledbetter later served as city marshal in Muskogee and Haskell as well.

This photograph of officers in the Choctaw Nation's Kiamitia County was taken in 1899 just before the bizarre sequence of events in which Sheriff James Usarey (at left) took over the duties of Judge Solomon Hotema (right) after the latter murdered his wife, daughter, and brother under the assumption that they were witches.

Oklahoma City patrolman John Dean joined the force in the 1890s and looked to be on course for a promising career in law enforcement before losing his job for political reasons. Months after being dismissed, he suffered a fractured skull when kicked by a frightened horse. He never quite recovered.

Often overlooked as a key player in the fight to rid Oklahoma Territory of the criminal element was the aggressive U.S. attorney Horace Speed, seen here in his Guthrie office with Deputy Marshal Chris Madsen (at right) in the 1890s.

Wa'tan'gaa or Black Coyote "set his feet in the white man's road," yet he was "a good natured fellow, thoroughly loyal and reliable in the discharge of his duties and always ready to execute his orders at whatever personal risk." He's seen here as tribal delegate in Washington sporting his sheriff's badge and a Harrison peace medal.

The assembled court at Tishomingo in the Chickasaw Nation, around 1898. With presiding judge Cornelius Hardy (at center) is future governor William H. Murray between deputy marshals Bill Evans (seated, at far-left) and Joe Maytubby (third from left). Legendary Ardmore lawman Buck Garrett stands in the back (second from right).

Deputy United States marshals assemble in front of the Federal Court House in Muskogee shortly after the "Great Fire" that destroyed half the city on February 23, 1899.

Cozad, a Kiowa, was Anadarko chief of police around the turn of the century. With the coming of Oklahoma statehood in 1907, a new chapter in the story of Oklahoma lawmen was about to be written.

If I Don't Get Killed in a Gunfight Soon . . . I'll Have to Go to Bed and Die like a Woman

(1900–1919)

Oklahoma continued its quick march into modernity during this period as the Wild West faded away. The Curtis Act of 1898 removed restrictions put in place by the Five Civilized Tribes to limit the development of towns, and subsequent development, in conjunction with a boom in railroad building, created many new towns in the first decades of the twentieth century. Law enforcement responded to this shift with great dexterity as many former deputy marshals were recruited to be chiefs of police around the Oklahoma and Indian territories. Most notable were Heck Thomas in Lawton, Bill Tilghman in Oklahoma City, and Buck Garrett at Ardmore.

The coming of statehood in 1907 and the maturation of the federal court system in Oklahoma essentially brought an end to the period in which the United States marshals and their deputies were the premier law enforcement agents. Statehood brought the final organization of counties in the state, and the county sheriffs took over many of the duties of the federal marshals, who were now free to focus on escorting prisoners, apprehending fugitives, and other duties.

Entering the law enforcement picture in this era were the prohibition agents, slangily referred to as "revenooers" by many of their targets. Although Indian Territory had always prohibited alcohol, Oklahoma Territory was wet, but the new state of Oklahoma codified prohibition into its constitution. These men rooted out illegal liquor production facilities and investigated the illegal distribution of alcohol. They generally enlisted the aid of the county sheriff when making raids.

Many who had seen its wilder days felt they'd witnessed the end of the Old West, especially when "Red" Kelly—the man who shot the man who shot Jesse James—was killed on an Oklahoma City street by policeman Joe Burnett. Yet despite Oklahoma's rapid growth and civilization, there was still plenty of work for lawmen because many people in Oklahoma, while on the whole a God-fearing, law-abiding populace, were still used to frontier justice and thus maintained a certain suspicion for the authorities and placed a premium on loyalty to their friends, neighbors, and fellow tribesmen.

Deputy U.S. marshals D. M. Webb, Paden Tolbert, and Gideon White pause in Vinita, seat of the Northern District court. Tolbert and White were involved in the capture of Ned Christie, and Tolbert later worked with Webb during a big roundup of Cherokee cattle rustlers near Spavinaw in 1902.

This portrait of Comanche Essapunnua dramatically illustrates the role many Indian Policemen played in their societies. Here Essapunnua, a U.S. Indian Policeman in Anadarko and a medicine man, wears his badge on his vest, but it's obscured by his other symbol of office, the feathered gourd.

Most police work was done by beat cops in the state's early cities because horses and wagons were too noisy to be sneaky. However, patrol wagons, like this one in Guthrie in 1900, were quite useful in chasing down fleeing bank robbers and fugitives.

Deputy U.S. Marshal Alonzo Campbell (left) with his brother Plez near Hodgen, Indian Territory, ride horseback in the densely forested Choctaw country in 1900.

Rolling Pony had been a member of the U.S. Indian Police for 10 years when this photograph was taken in 1900. That same day, however, he said it would be his last because the agent made him release 10 of his 11 wives (an obvious sign of his status). He is pictured with the wife he chose to keep.

Shawnee-Cherokee John Chamberlain spent many years in close association with the U.S. Indian Police, but he only served one year as a deputy U.S. marshal. He made several arrests that year, but on one occasion had to escort a close friend to jail. He was so overcome with pity he knew he wasn't cut out for the job.

African-American Deputy U.S. Marshals (left to right) Amos Maytubby, Zeke Miller, Neely Factor, and Bob Fortune near Deadman's Crossing. They collared two murderers and two horse thieves on that particular outing, around 1900.

Mounted deputy U.S. marshals pose near Immaculate Conception Church in Fort Smith during a reunion of Judge Isaac Parker's former employees, around 1901.

White-bearded Benjamin Franklin Hackett presides over an assembly of his deputies and other men at his office in McAlester. Hackett was named United States Marshal for the Central District of the Indian Territory in 1901 and was known to be unusually meddlesome in political matters.

Former Cherokee councilman T. Wyman Thompson (shown here ca. 1901) had a varied career spanning nearly 30 years, including service as a deputy U.S. marshal and undersheriff of Mayes County.

Deputy U.S. Marshal William Perry Pound (left) came from the cowboy life in Texas and worked mainly in the Choctaw Nation. After retirement he was known as a remarkably apt water-well driller around the new state.

Assembled peace officers of Comanche County and Lawton soon after the land opening by lottery in 1901. Lawton's ordinances were decided on democratic principles, but few restrictions were placed on gambling and drinking, and shooting out lights and windows was quite common.

This secluded house on the open prairie was the scene of a shoot-out which cost the lives of Caddo County sheriff Frank Smith and deputy George Beck. Three highwaymen led by Bert Casey, one of Oklahoma's most bloodthirsty criminals, murdered the lawmen, robbed their bodies, and made their escape.

In the Choctaw Nation, the sheriff and his deputies were obliged to mete out the punishments sent down by the courts. According to Section 17 of the Choctaw Constitution, the penalty for stealing cattle was one hundred lashes on the bare back, as freedman Amos Shoat learned all too well in 1901.

Soon after the Kiowa, Comanche, and Caddo lands were opened to settlement in 1901, residents of Lawton beseeched the Indian agent at Anadarko to help protect the city from predatory gamblers. The agent had no authority to intervene, but Indian Policemen like these were on hand to protect Indians in the vicinity.

U.S. Marshal Bill Fossett (left) had a friendship of more than 60 years with Joe Grimes (right) and stood by his old pal when fellow Republicans tried to block Democrat Grimes' appointment as his deputy, around 1902.

Former Apache chief Geronimo became a celebrity during his imprisonment at Fort Sill. He was even allowed to make appearances at public events. Here he rides alongside Anadarko city marshal Frank Hefley in the city's 1903 Independence Day parade.

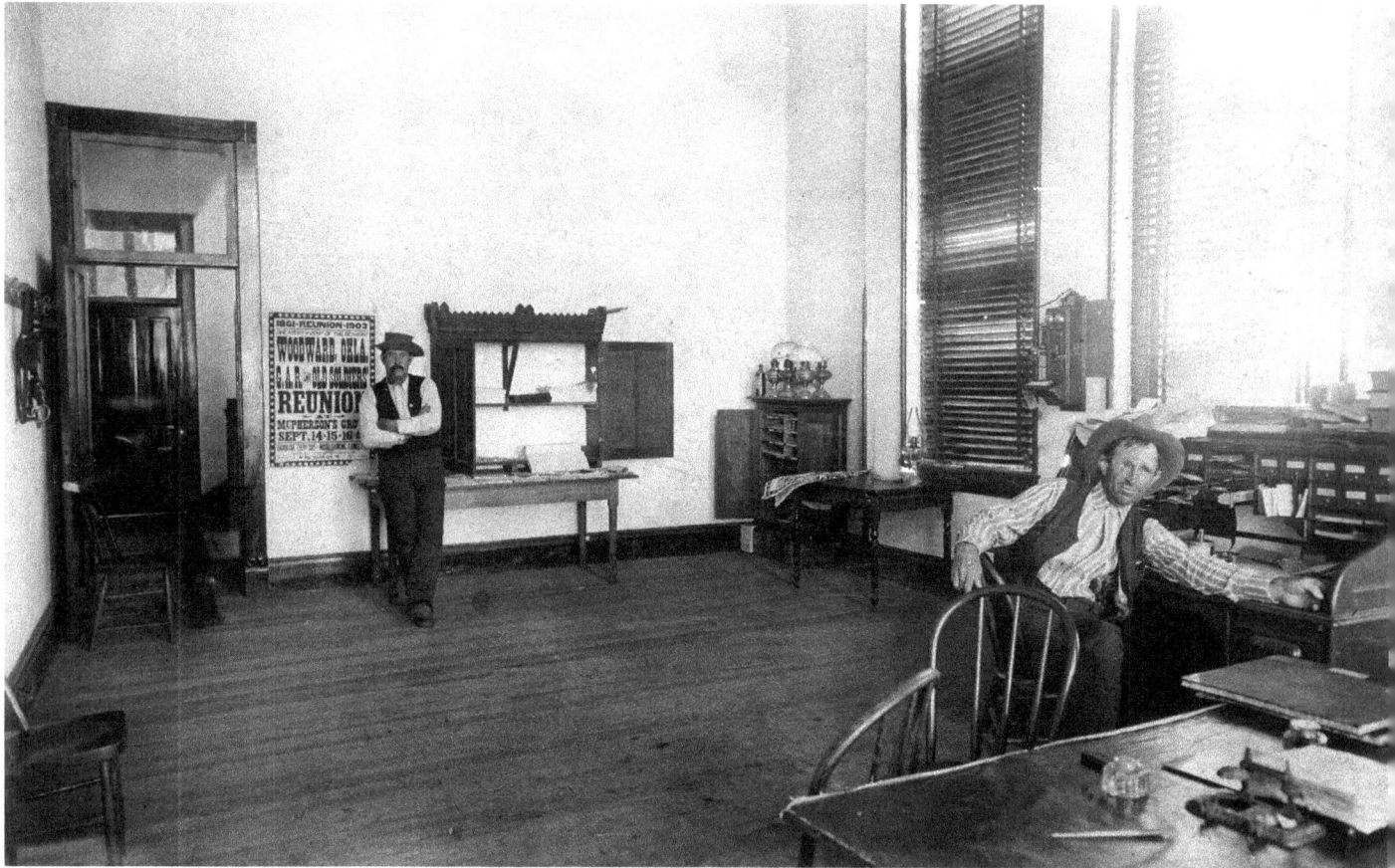

Scene in the Woodward County sheriff's office in 1903. The bill on the back wall advertises a reunion to be held in mid-September for veterans of the Civil War.

Orris H. Emerick, an 1889er, won a highly politicized and contested race to become Oklahoma City chief of police in 1903, whereupon he cracked a burglary case on his first day at work. Having failed to win reelection, he moved to Enid to join his brother in a moving-and-storage company—one that still operates today.

This gathering of Oklahoma County sheriffs was likely photographed during the term of its most prominent member, William Tilghman (standing, third from left), who served as Lincoln County sheriff from 1900 to 1904.

Bohemian draft dodger John Hubatka was one of four original Oklahoma City policemen in 1890 and went on to a 40-year "violent bullet-torn career." Eulogized for his fearlessness in the face of danger, it was said of him, "The bullet was never molded that could touch Hubatka." He died in his sleep at 66.

Twenty-nine prisoners from Oklahoma and Indian territories take one last gasp of free air before boarding freight cars. Until the state penitentiary was built in 1909, territorial prisoners were transported to federal prisons in Kansas and Ohio.

Prisoners ready for transport peer through freight car doors. Prisoner transport was just another part of the job for deputy U.S. marshals, and situations alternated between boredom and danger.

"Few men were more widely known in Oklahoma," it was said of D. F. Smith. Ultimately a political party hack, "Fatty" Smith was sheriff of Beaver County in "No Man's Land" in the 1880s and was appointed first sheriff of Blaine County and later territorial oil inspector. He was elected to the legislature in 1904.

Members of the Lawton Police Department (from the left): Heck Thomas, Leka Hammon, Harry Foster, Bill Bruce, and Colonel J. W. Hawkins. Aging Heck Thomas was brought in to tame the wild town, but still Hawkins was shot and killed by a local newspaper editor during a political rally in 1904.

City Marshal Washington Williams (at back, far-left) appears with the first town council of Boley, Oklahoma, around 1905. Williams' predecessor in the all-black town was ex–Deputy U.S. Marshal Dick Shaver, who was gunned down in an ambush by members of the outlaw Simmons Gang.

Sixty mounted Oklahoma City policemen lead what is likely the parade in honor of William Jennings Bryan, who was visiting in 1905. Bryan had run for president in 1896 and 1900 and would run again in 1908. Despite such a large force, the department did not regularly use mounted police because of the unlikelihood of a stealthy approach upon criminals.

Despite the boyish innocence exhibited by Epworth University batboy George Goff in 1906, he would later serve two frightening terms as Oklahoma county sheriff, during which he created his own paramilitary "Civil Guards," registered gun owners, and trampled civil liberties.

Seen here around 1907 are officials from Washita County, including Sheriff Neal Morrison (seated at bottom, center), who was wounded in the same gunfight that killed two of his deputies in June 1900 as they pursued members of the Casey Gang near Cloud Chief.

Members of the "Federal Official Family" gathered on the courthouse steps in Muskogee to welcome Oklahoma into the union on November 16, 1907. Most notable in this assembly is Deputy Marshal "Bud" Ledbetter (large man in the front row) and famous Deputy Marshal Bass Reeves (far left, second row).

Dapper Charles Post won election as Oklahoma City chief of police amid the sweep of reform in 1907. For a time his "Flying Squadron" of raiders attacked vice in every corner of the city, but eventually reform fervor cooled. Post went on to a 40-year career as a detective and investigator.

For a while the Oklahoma County Jail was jokingly known as "Mrs. Meadows' Home" when Lila Meadows spent nearly a year in relatively luxurious custody during her trial for the murder of her husband, James, in 1907. She was acquitted in 1908, but her paramour, Rudolph, received a life sentence in 1910 for pulling the trigger.

McCurtain County's first elected sheriff was Tom Graham. The dense forests and proximity to other states made it a fugitive's paradise, but Graham's specialty was fearlessly rooting out the many well-hidden moonshiners in the area. He was even greeted with a parade and brass band in Idabel after a big raid in 1911.

The assembled force of the Chickasha Police Department pose with their Black Maria in 1908. A year later the department would be rocked by the murder of Chief Emmett Goodwin by fellow officer William Thomas after an argument over the efficacy of the force.

In April 1909, a sizable mob in Ada stormed the jail, removed the men imprisoned for the murder of former Deputy Marshal A. A. Bobbitt, and strung them up in a nearby stable. Though most details are still shrouded in mystery, "Deacon" Jim Miller (at left) was undoubtedly the triggerman.

Oklahoma State Penitentiary guard Sam Hargis stands watch from a crude tower during the construction of the permanent structure in May 1909. Formerly housed in Kansas, Oklahoma prisoners were brought to McAlester where they first constructed the stockade seen here and later the fortress patterned after Leavenworth prison.

Okfuskee County deputy Bailey Wilson (left) and Sheriff William McCulley (right) embark for McAlester to deliver the county's first inmates (in handcuffs, and one of whom is inexplicably gloved) to the Oklahoma State Penitentiary, around 1909.

Hugh Martin was the first elected sheriff after statehood in Woods County and later served as a deputy U.S. marshal in the area. As sheriff he presided over the investigation into Woods County's first homicide in 1910 when the lifeless body of Miss Mabel Oakes was discovered in Alva's opera house.

Perhaps no one in Oklahoma lived as colorful a life as Frank Canton. After a 10-year career of robbery and murder as Joe Horner, his real name, he changed his name to Canton and took a new identity as a cattle rancher, later becoming a sheriff and one of the Regulators in Wyoming's Johnson County War. Later he was a deputy U.S. marshal, a Klondike prospector, Pawnee County deputy, and ultimately a general in the Oklahoma National Guard. For his service in law enforcement, he was pardoned late in life by the governor of Texas when he confessed to being the outlaw Horner.

Bartlesville police detective J. R. Spurrier, around 1910. Spurrier contracted Spanish influenza during his World War I service. He recovered, but the disease took his Osage wife and his parents took custody of his children in order to gain control of their allotments.

Dubbed "the Prince of Hangmen," George Maledon served nearly a quarter-century as the hangman for "Hangin' Judge" Isaac Parker. Though difficult to verify all his executions, it is believed from 66 to 88 men were "legally passported into the arms of death."

Seen here in 1910, imposing six-foot-five John C. West defended law and order in the Cherokee Nation for more than 40 years as a deputy U.S. marshal and captain of Light Horsemen, often making it his personal mission to rein in the villainous activities of the Starr family.

Harkening back to the earliest days when Oklahoma City was divided by two distinct city governments, this old jail (seen in 1910) at South Broadway and Second, was the "Southtown" city jail. Recidivist badman Clyde Maddox was nearly taken from the jail and lynched before soldiers intervened to protect him.

If the public had any doubts as to the utility of the Oklahoma City Police Department's new motorcycle squad in 1910, they were erased months later when patrolman G. E. Johnson leapt from his speeding cycle onto a runaway horse on Harvey Avenue, halting the horse, and saving the mother and child in the buggy behind.

Although he was actually a "wet," new Oklahoma City mayor Whit Grant decided to strictly enforce the city's prohibition laws, hoping the pressure would lubricate the dry town. To that end, he brought in the toughest lawman in Oklahoma as police chief, Bill Tilghman, seen here with pal Chris Madsen (at left) around 1912.

Though little is known about his career, former Deputy U.S. Marshal Pardee Harmon (at right) spent his twilight years raising horses for rancher Lute Jackson near Cornish in Chickasaw country. Curiously, while on a trip to Fort Smith, Jackson's mother made fast friends and even exchanged recipes with Belle Starr.

James Montgomery Dillon, constable of Coal County for a number of years. Though not a familiar office today, constables were attached to and executed the decrees of local justices of the peace. Mainly that involved civil action, but they could enforce all laws governing their jurisdiction.

Logan County sheriff John Mahoney was a tough lawman. In 1913 he rescued a prisoner from a lynching by whisking him out of town in a car with a mob in hot pursuit. When their car ran out of gas they ran on foot, but farmers soon gave chase, so he flagged down a passing train and got the prisoner safely away to a hidden location.

Grady County lawmen display the results of a successful raid in the war on moonshine near the jail and courthouse in Chickasha.

William McClure, Captain of the Choctaw Light Horse, around 1915.

Captain Jim Turner of the Choctaw Light Horse, around 1915.

Dewey County lawmen display their latest victory over moonshiners, around 1915. "Uncle Joe" Ventioner stands at right displaying his famous pearl-handled Colt revolvers. He had a long and illustrious career with the U.S. Marshals and Dewey County, even serving as jailer into his 70s.

After ex-outlaw Al Jennings made the favorable film *Beating Back* in 1914, his old foe Bill Tilghman decided to set the record straight by helming *Passing of the Oklahoma Outlaws* a year later. Here he is seen (right) at the film's premiere.

Woodward County sheriff Ed Durant (reclining at desk) shoots the breeze in his office in 1917. Two years earlier he was seriously wounded in an ambush by a deranged man who fired several rounds into his midsection. Durant received prompt medical treatment and having been in possession of "a robust constitution" soon recovered.

Steve Buchanan was well known throughout southeastern Oklahoma. As special peace officer for the expansive Dierks Coal and Lumber Company for more than 40 years, he roamed Le Flore County guarding payroll, breaking up fights, and generally keeping the peace in the many company towns.

A Choctaw member of the United States Indian Police, around 1918.

Britton city marshal Luther Bishop (at center) poses with officers of Britton State Bank in 1917. Bishop later excelled as a plainclothes detective for the Oklahoma City Police Department in the 1920s, specializing in nabbing bank robbers.

Oklahoma County jailers demonstrate how newspapers were used to smuggle narcotics into the jail for use by addict inmates, a relatively common occurrence around 1919. Confiscated drugs were once destroyed, but during World War I, they were collected and turned over to the Red Cross for use on wounded soldiers.

Every Home in Oklahoma Has Its Hootch

(1920–1959)

With the passage of the Volstead Act and the subsequent arrival of national prohibition in 1919, federal prohibition agents grew in number and their duties and workload greatly expanded. The effectiveness of bootleggers and organized criminals varied around the country as the illicit trade in liquor became lucrative, but in Oklahoma bootleggers and smugglers had always been a presence and their level of organization and infiltration into mainstream society (often including local law enforcement) frustrated federal agents assigned to the state. Prohibition remained in force until 1959—25 years after the rest of the country moved on—and enforcement of these laws remained an important focus among Oklahoma lawmen.

Lawmen were also challenged by the oil boom towns, which could appear quickly in a previously undeveloped part of a county or cause an existing community to swell to ten times its normal size. County sheriffs faced acute problems as the large numbers of young men with large amounts of disposable income attracted prostitution, gambling, and bootlegging, creating a law enforcement crisis in places all across the state. Particularly raucous was the town of Cromwell, so overcome with crime that citizens coaxed aging ex–Deputy Marshal Bill Tilghman out of retirement to head their police force and clean up the town. Tilghman, who had tamed Dodge City, Kansas, and Perry, Oklahoma, could not relive his past glory. He was murdered in 1924 by a crooked prohibition agent in a city street.

Despite the continuing maturation of Oklahoma, the state still had a reputation for lawlessness, and criminal gangs still terrorized Oklahoma and the Southwest. Banks swelled by farm subsidies, oil money, and Indian payments made delicious targets for the likes of Henry Starr, Bonnie and Clyde, and other desperadoes. These highly mobile gangs only increased in activity during the hard times of the Great Depression, which saw the appearance of Pretty Boy Floyd and Machine Gun Kelly. To combat this threat, the Oklahoma Bureau of Investigation was created in 1925 with the authority to pursue criminals anywhere inside state borders. They were quite effective.

Like the rest of the country, Oklahoma's municipal police and the newly created (in 1937) Highway Patrol brought modern practices to her largest cities in the post–World War II era. Improvements in training and an emphasis on public safety radically altered the way policemen performed their duties during this period.

Portly but austere, J. E. Brants was assigned to Oklahoma as a special federal prohibition enforcement officer, around 1920. He would be very busy.

Federal officer Joe Foster (center) is flanked by Oklahoma County sheriff Ben Dancey (right) and deputy Luther Bishop (left) as they prepare to pour 2,000 gallons of bootleg whiskey into Oklahoma City's sewer system, around 1921.

Sheriff Ben Dancey (center) and deputies bust up a still in Oklahoma County in the 1920s. Prohibition was nothing new to Oklahoma, but the Eighteenth Amendment increased enforcement efforts. One federal officer complained, "The stills are thick as flies here."

Bill Aldridge fronts a no-nonsense image during his days as a Seminole County deputy in the 1920s. He had to. In the wake of an oil boom, which saw the county's population increase fourfold, his jurisdiction was home to some of the most notorious locales in the state, among them Cromwell and Bishop's Alley.

The home of retired Seminole Light Horseman Concharty (seated), around the 1920s. This is probably the same Concharty who was among the last of the Seminoles to leave Florida in 1858.

Prohibition agents seize yet another illicit liquor still in Oklahoma County, around the 1920s.

Pawnee Indian Policeman Sam Horse Chief confronts modernity, around 1925.

Following Spread: Officers of Mayes County, (left to right) Deputy Willis Thompson, Undersheriff T. Wyman Thompson, Sheriff Charles M. Kelly, and Deputy Cleo Callison display the fruits of their investigations—stills and moonshine—in front of the County Courthouse in 1928.

Oklahoma County officers, including Luther Bishop (at right), in the early 1920s. Bishop was later an Oklahoma State Bureau of Investigation agent, but about a year later, in 1926, he was murdered in his home. Investigators first called it an assassination, but focus later turned to his wife, Edith. She was acquitted and the case was never solved.

In the spring of 1931, former deputy U.S. marshal and bank robber Emmett Dalton made this photograph during a final trip to Oklahoma to visit the graves of his family, including brothers Bob and Grat. Despite sustaining 23 gunshot wounds, Emmett became the sole survivor of the Coffeyville raid in which his brothers were killed. He served his prison time and finally became wealthy in California real estate.

McClain County sheriff Orin Johnston (third from left) and his deputies are seen around 1932, after busting up a well-camouflaged liquor operation outside Purcell.

Hiding his wounded right hand, Kansas State Prison escapee Lew Bechtel stands next to Delaware County sheriff Carl Curtis after his recapture on June 2, 1933. Eleven prisoners escaped a few days earlier, but Curtis caught up to Bechtel as he ate lunch in a farmhouse. His captor allowed him to finish his meal.

Seen here during his days as Carter County sheriff (1935–1942), Floyd Randolph was elected after a 25-year career as a rodeo star at the 101 Ranch Wild West Show. His election campaign was undoubtedly aided by his talented and famous wife, Florence—the first woman to do a handstand from a saddle horn.

Sporting a pith helmet, an Oklahoma City traffic cop gives a group of boys a stern talking-to in the late 1930s. Perhaps the lecture dealt with passing streetcars, which still posed an ever-present danger to unwary pedestrians of the era.

Although he held the office only three years, former U.S. Marshal Evett D. Nix remained a celebrity well into the 1930s when he became popular promotng his version of events in a book called *Oklahombres: Particularly the Wilder Ones.*

Concerned about the state's deadly roads, Governor Marland formed the Oklahoma State Highway Patrol to enforce a slew of new traffic laws in 1937. Oklahoma drivers had never had licenses or rules, so the patrolmen manning this first fleet of vehicles were trained to be especially courteous.

Fifty years after its founding, Guthrie fielded a fully modern urban police force, seen here in 1937.

Following Spread: Elijah Gabbert was nearly 50 years old when he began his 30-year law enforcement career as a deputy sheriff in Pittsburg County, contending with the occasional escaped inmate from the state prison in McAlester. For the last half of that career, he was a constable, serving papers from his horse and buggy until 1937.

In 1937, Woodward County sheriff's officers display a huge still and all the fixin's—the results of the largest liquor raid in the county's history.

"We shot 'em, threw 'em, anything to break the bottles," said Woodward County sheriff Elmer Nelson after the destruction of 2,000 pints of bonded whiskey at a dump east of Woodward around 1938.

At 7:30 A.M., August 20, 1940, the Oklahoma City Police Department became fully mobilized using these radio patrol cars and doing away with downtown foot patrols. Veteran Captain Lloyd White was moved to resign, saying, "I consider many of the chief's plans impractical and believe they are tearing up the department."

Created by Oklahoma City mayor O. A. Cargill in 1923, the Flat-Foot Four, a barbershop quartet made up of Oklahoma City policemen, won the national barbershop quartet singing championship at the World's Fair in New York in 1940. Carrying firearms in this image, they sing for NBC Radio.

Late in life the old Guardsman Chris Madsen became a technical advisor on many Hollywood movie sets. One protégé was a young Roy Rogers, seen here with the 89-year-old Madsen at the premiere of *Young Bill Hickok,* October 21, 1940.

Delf "Jelly" Bryce was a fearless Oklahoma City cop and blazing quick shot in the 1930s, ultimately becoming a successful FBI agent and later training new agents in the art of marksmanship. Famous for his ability to drop a coin from shoulder height and shoot it before it hit the floor, he became legendary for the speed and accuracy with which he could draw and fire.

Oklahoma City police chief L. J. Hilbert and a highway patrolman congratulate a young patrolman at the Kiwanis Junior Police awards in 1946. Since the 1920s, the Kiwanis Club had sponsored a student safety program, which evolved into the Junior Police and operated somewhat like crossing guards.

Frank Eaton was truly a living legend when he was photographed in Perkins at the age of 91. Eaton learned to use a gun at a young age and earned the nickname Pistol Pete for his marksmanship. He became a deputy for Judge Parker at the age of 17 and vowed to kill his father's six murderers. They were all dead within 10 years.

Mayes County sheriff Ralph Willcutt investigates at the murder scene of County Attorney Jack Burris in 1952. Officials suspected bootleggers were behind what's believed to be the first time an elected official was assassinated in Oklahoma. The case remains unsolved.

L. L. "Slim" Weaver displays the trophies of a successful liquor raid in December 1953. With the large number of resorts and vacation homes on Grand Lake creating a demand, illegal liquor was never in short supply in Mayes County.

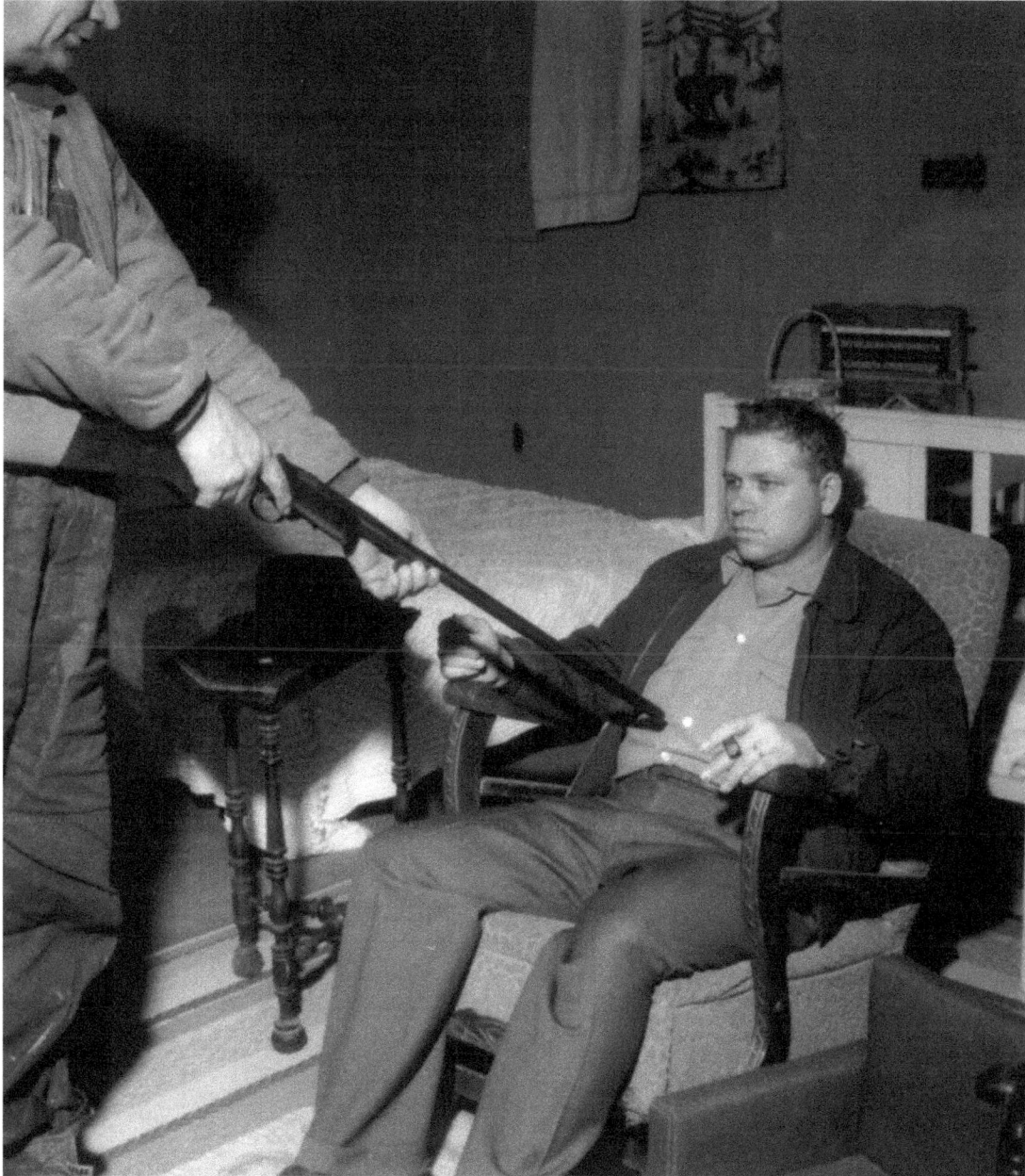

An unidentified lawman, possibly an Oklahoma County sheriff's officer, detains a suspect in his Oklahoma City home early in the 1950s.

Prohibition officers display a confiscated still discovered in an Oklahoma City garage.

An Oklahoma City policeman collects funds from a parking meter outside City Hall in 1954. The invention of the parking meter in 1935 is generally credited to Cityan Carl Magee.

Despite moderate resistance, the Oklahoma City Council made the decision to allow women to serve on the police force in 1955. Six women were selected—three housewives and three secretaries—to work traffic enforcement downtown.

An Oklahoma City police major from the Traffic Division explains the carefully devised traffic routes for the Southwest American Exposition at the Fairgrounds in April 1956. Despite his best efforts, organizers were unprepared as hundreds of thousands came to the weeklong event including more than 100,000 on the last day.

An Oklahoma City policeman investigates a trove of confiscated weapons and other evidence on the front seat of his scout car.

An Oklahoma City policeman shows off his scout car in 1956. In March, the Scout Car Division nabbed 53 burglars, the highest monthly total ever achieved by the force to that date.

Oklahoma City police officers restrain an arrestee in the rear of their squad car in 1957.

Civil rights champions including Clara Luper (center) leave Oklahoma City police headquarters after their release from custody following sit-ins in 1958. Police and protesters mutually respected and cooperated with each other, and Luper formed a lasting bond with downtown officer and future chief I. G. Purser.

Oklahoma City police work the scene of a car accident at Shartel and Reno in 1957.

A new recruit undergoes firearms training for the Oklahoma City Police Department. In 1956, the department introduced new, stricter requirements including height, weight, and education standards.

Notes on the Photographs

These notes, listed by page number, attempt to include all aspects known of the photographs. Each of the photographs is identified by the page number, photograph's title or description, photographer and collection, archive, and call or box number when applicable. Although every attempt was made to collect all data, in some cases complete data may have been unavailable due to the age and condition of some of the photographs and records.

127 **BAILEY WILSON, WILLIAM MCCULLEY, AND GROUP**
Western History Collection
University of Oklahoma
Payne10

128 **HUGH MARTIN**
Waynoka Historical Society
Hugh Martin Jr--

129 **FRANK CANTON**
Western History Collection
University of Oklahoma
Dale191

130 **J. R. SPURRIER**
Courtesy of the Oklahoma
Historical Society
22251.23

131 **HANGMAN GEORGE MALEDON**
Fort Smith National
Historic Site National Park
Service
20071026112236

132 **JOHN C. WEST WITH FELLOW OFFICERS**
Courtesy of the Oklahoma
Historical Society
4266-C

133 **THE OLD "SOUTHTOWN" CITY JAIL, 1910**
Courtesy of the Oklahoma
Historical Society
3409

134 **POLICE DEPARTMENT MOTORCYCLE SQUAD**
Courtesy of the Oklahoma
Historical Society
9410

135 **CHRIS MADSEN AND BILL TILGHMAN, 1912**
Courtesy of the Oklahoma
Historical Society
5608

136 **PARDEE HARMON WITH HORSES**
Courtesy of the Oklahoma
Historical Society
17583

137 **JAMES MONTGOMERY DILLON**
Courtesy of the Oklahoma
Historical Society
23281

138 **LOGAN COUNTY SHERIFF JOHN MAHONEY**
Courtesy of the Oklahoma
Historical Society
18027

139 **GRADY COUNTY LAWMEN AFTER MOONSHINE RAID**
Western History Collection
University of Oklahoma
Munn89

140 **WILLIAM MCCLURE**
Courtesy of the Oklahoma
Historical Society
5873

141 **CAPTAIN JIM TURNER**
Courtesy of the Oklahoma
Historical Society
4962

142 **DEWEY COUNTY LAWMEN WITH CONTRABAND**
Western History Collection
University of Oklahoma
DeweyCounty11

143 **BILL TILGHMAN AT FILM PREMIERE**
Courtesy of the Oklahoma
Historical Society
12369

145 **SHERIFF ED DURANT AT HIS DESK, 1917**
Plains Indians & Pioneers
Museum
1967.017.003

146 **PEACE OFFICER STEVE BUCHANAN**
Courtesy of the Oklahoma
Historical Society
16951

147 **CHOCTAW MEMBER OF U.S. INDIAN POLICE**
Courtesy of the Oklahoma
Historical Society
2431-123

148 **BRITTON CITY MARSHAL LUTHER BISHOP**
Courtesy of the Oklahoma
Historical Society
13648

150 **SMUGGLING BY NEWSPAPER**
Courtesy of the Oklahoma
Historical Society
13641-1

152 **J. E. BRANTS**
Courtesy of the Oklahoma
Historical Society
120

153 **OFFICERS WITH PROHIBITION CONTRABAND**
Courtesy of the Oklahoma
Historical Society
13645

155 **SHERIFF BEN DANCEY AND DEPUTIES WITH CONTRABAND**
Courtesy of the Oklahoma
Historical Society
13639

156 **DEPUTY BILL ALDRIDGE, 1920S**
Courtesy of the Oklahoma
Historical Society
19222.40

157 **SEMINOLE LIGHT HORSEMAN CONCHARTY**
Courtesy of the Oklahoma
Historical Society
16303

158 **ILLEGAL LIQUOR STILL**
Courtesy of the Oklahoma
Historical Society
13643

159 **SAM HORSE CHIEF**
Courtesy of the Oklahoma
Historical Society
3700

160 **OFFICERS OF MAYES COUNTY**
Courtesy of the Terry Lamar
Collection

162 **LUTHER BISHOP WITH FELLOW OFFICERS**
Courtesy of the Oklahoma
Historical Society
13638

163 **EMMETT DALTON**
Western History Collection
University of Oklahoma
Dale25

165 **ORIN JOHNSTON AND DEPUTIES WITH CONTRABAND**
Courtesy of the Oklahoma
Historical Society
17392

166 **SHERIFF CARL CURTIS WITH ESCAPEE LEW BECHTEL**
Courtesy of the Oklahoma
Historical Society
21171.36

LIST OF REFERENCES

Burton, Arthur T. *Black Gun, Silver Star: The Life and Legend of Frontier Marshal Bass Reeves.* Lincoln: University of Nebraska Press, 2006.

Burton, Arthur T. *Black, Red, and Deadly: Black and Indian Gunfighters of the Indian Territory, 1870–1907.* Austin, Tex.: Eakin Press, 1991.

Daily Arkansas Gazette. Little Rock: W. E. Woodruff, Jr., 1866.

Daily Oklahoman. Oklahoma City: Oklahoma Newspaper Co., 1894.

Dallas Morning News. Dallas: A. H. Belo & Co., 1885.

Fulbright, Jim. *W. D. "Bill" Fossett: Pioneer and Peace Officer.* Goodlettsville, Tenn.: Mid-South Publ., 2002.

Haines, J. D. *Wiley G. Haines: Frontier U.S. Deputy Marshal.* Austin, Tex.: Eakin Press, 2002.

Jones, William Frank. *The Experiences of a Deputy U.S. Marshall of the Indian Territory.* N.p., 1937.

Kansas City Star. Kansas City, Mo.: Kansas City Star Co., 1880.

Mooney, James, and Ervin W. Read. *The Ghost-Dance Religion and the Sioux Outbreak of 1890.* Washington, D.C.: Government Printing Office, 1896.

Nix, Evett Dumas. *Oklahombres: Particularly the Wilder Ones.* St. Louis: Eden Publishing House, 1929.

Owens, Ron (Ronald J.). *Jelly Bryce: Legendary Lawman.* Paducah, Ky.: Turner Publishing Company, 2003.

Shirley, Glenn. *Buckskin and Spurs: A Gallery of Frontier Rogues and Heroes.* New York: Hastings House, 1958.

———. *Guardian of the Law: The Life and Time of William Matthew Tilghman (1854–1924).* Austin, Tex.: Eakin Press, 1988.

———. *Heck Thomas: Frontier Marshal.* Norman: University of Oklahoma Press, 1981, 1962.

———. *Law West of Fort Smith: A History of Frontier Justice in the Indian Territory, 1834–1896.* New York: H. Holt, 1968, 1957.

———. *West of Hell's Fringe: Crime, Criminals, and Federal Peace Officers in Oklahoma Territory, 1889–1907.* Norman: University of Oklahoma Press, 1978.

United States. *Annual Report of the Board of Indian Commissioners to the Secretary of the Interior.* Washington, D.C.: Government Printing Office, 1870–1932.

HISTORIC PHOTOS OF
OKLAHOMA LAWMEN

Oklahoma has a famously violent past and equally famous lawmen who brought peace and order to this once lawless land. Thanks to Oklahoma's relative youth the exploits of many of these lawmen were caught on camera. *Historic Photos of Oklahoma Lawmen* presents the many faces and phases of law enforcement in Oklahoma throughout its early history up through the 1950s.

Inside are images of the Five Civilized Tribes' brave Light Horsemen, the scouts and Dog Soldiers of the West, and the federal marshals who ranged Indian Territory in service to the court of Fort Smith's "hangin' judge" Isaac Parker. Here, too, are the state's earliest municipal policemen and county sheriffs who arrived to protect and defend the state's cities and boom towns.

Larry Johnson holds a degree in history from Southern Nazarene University, a library degree from the University of Oklahoma, and a cherished certificate in Nuclear Disaster Preparedness from FEMA.

Johnson is a frequent contributor to *Info* magazine and is the author of *Historic Photos of Oklahoma, Historic Photos of Oklahoma City,* and *Historic Photos of Harry S. Truman,* all available from Turner Publishing. He is a reference librarian for the Metropolitan Library System where he maintains the Oklahoma Room and the Oklahoma Images database.

Johnson lives in Oklahoma City where he spins Raymond Scott records on his 10-watt pirate radio station.

WWW.TURNERPUBLISHING.COM

www.ingramcontent.com/pod-product-compliance
Lightning Source LLC
Chambersburg PA
CBHW061227150426
42812CB00054BA/2536